Just imagine...

What you'd be able to achieve
if you knew
that you cannot fail?

#Educatia #MarioBeky

LEO - Learning organizer

Everyone of us has incredible potential! In those very moments when we decide to use all of our energy to achieve our full potential we open ourselves to endless opportunities.
We, the people, can create incredible things and reach almost any goal no matter what obstacles we encounter!

This is Organizer will change how you set and achieve your goals. It shows you how to map out the different parts of your day, how to find the required motivation and gives you strategies to help you make your dreams a reality. And the best thing about the LEO Organizer is that it's completely customized for you: taking into account your age, your expectations and your abilities!

Alexander the Great, Albert Einstein and Thomas A. Edison have shown us how our lives can change when we define and reach for our goals. Take action now and take the first step toward achieving anything you desire. Once you start, you will see how your life will change!

I, ____________________ (your name) , am willing to use my full potential to reach my goals.

____

date and your signature

LEO - Learning organizer offers me more than a **Plan.** *Motivational Quotes* will boost me right in the morning. I will remind myself on what is **My Big Goal** and I will also set up my **Goals for today.** From now on I'll have my **Tests and exams** under control because I'm the manager of my testing schedule. I know that Fortune favors not only the bold but first of all those who are prepared. Therefore I'll prepare **Things I need** in advance to make my day a successful one. Learning organizer will also remind me about the list of **People I want to meet** along with the subjects of our meetings. It is told that if we want to get to close to our goals we must overcome at least ❶ fear a day. **My mentor** is the right person who will help me to meet the **Challenges.** Do I know **What do I need to do to make this day great?** Absolutely, yes & **LEO** - will help me to create a **100% successful strategy.**

Wise words will encourage me in following my dreams. After a day in the school I'll remind me about all **My successes** and **Incredible ideas** I had today. **Preparation / learning plan** is here to organize my thoughts and save my precious time for me to relax and have more fun afterwards. If I spend first half from day's 24 hour cycle on recupering the energy (sleeping, eating, relaxing, etc.) I can use the other half for efficient work. An **Efficiency of** my **12 hour cycle** is remarkable. I work very hard on achieving my dreams and goals but I will focus even more and do what ever it takes to reach unreachable. I'm dividing my day into several smaller challenges that are easier to handle and this creates for me more opportunities to achieve the moment of success. I can't wait to do **My day's evaluation** in the evening because I'll give myself a **Reward for meeting all my objectives**. I'm an effective and persistent hard worker therefore it's easy for me to sum up everything **I'm grateful for**. The experiences, accomplishments and meetings with new people are helping me to be closer to my dreams. It's always wise to remind me on **What I learned today** because it will also show me **How good I'm prepared for the next awesome day**.

LEO - Learning organizer is fantastic companion! It's giving me the helping hand to plan a road to my goals in every detail. I **Understand my possibilities** therefore I recognize my strengths and use them to reach my full potential. **My mind is free** because I have under control not only myself but also the **Things I need today** in my school bag. I'm focusing on what I want to achieve and choosing the correct **Strategies for reaching the goals.** It's pleasure to watch my **Evaluation and improvement.** However, this is just the beginning. There is more to come and I can't wait to reach after everything I desire. Now I believe, now I know that I can take this unbelievable chance with both of my hands and use all **#MyFullPotential.**

Date __ / __ / ____

"This is my day!"

Main Goals ☐ ☐ ☐

My Big Goal (long-term)

Additional tasks

Exams / tests 1. 2. 3.

Things I need — school supplies ☐ ☐ ☐

People I want to meet — name/reason ☐ ☐ ☐

Today's challenge ☐

My mentor's tasks 1. ☐ 2. ☐

What do I need to do to make this day great?

Today's successes

Incredible ideas

Preparation / learning plan

4:00 pm ☐

5:00 pm ☐

6:00 pm ☐

7:00 pm ☐

8:00 pm ☐

9:00 pm ☐

Efficiency of my 12 hour cycle

hours %

12 3 6 9

How do I evaluate my today's efforts? 0 25% 50% 75% 100%

Reward for meeting all my objectives

I am grateful for...

Today I learned...

How good am I prepared for the next day? 0 25% 50% 75% 100%

Date __/__/____

- long-term preparation is the key for the improvement -

Main Goals ☐ ☐ ☐

My Big Goal (long-term)

Additional tasks

Exams / tests 1. 2. 3.

Things I need — school supplies ☐ ☐ ☐

People I want to meet — name/reason ☐ ☐ ☐

Today's challenge ☐

My mentor's tasks 1. ☐ 2. ☐

What do I need to do to make this day great?

Today's successes

Incredible ideas

Preparation / learning plan

4:00 pm ☐

5:00 pm ☐

6:00 pm ☐

7:00 pm ☐

8:00 pm ☐

9:00 pm ☐

Efficiency of my 12 hour cycle

hours %

12 3 6 9

How do I evaluate my today's efforts? 0 25% 50% 75% 100%

Reward for meeting all my objectives

I am grateful for...

Today I learned...

How good am I prepared for the next day? 0 25% 50% 75% 100%

Date __/__/____ ____________

"Today I feel great!"

Main Goals ☐ ☐ ☐

My Big Goal (long-term)

Additional tasks

Exams / tests 1. 2. 3.

Things I need — school supplies ☐ ☐ ☐

People I want to meet — name/reason ☐ ☐ ☐

Today's challenge ☐

My mentor's tasks 1. ☐ 2. ☐

What do I need to do to make this day great?

Today's successes

Incredible ideas

Preparation / learning plan

4:00 pm ☐

5:00 pm ☐

6:00 pm ☐

7:00 pm ☐

8:00 pm ☐

9:00 pm ☐

Efficiency of my 12 hour cycle

hours %

12 3 6 9

How do I evaluate my today's efforts? 0 25% 50% 75% 100%

Reward for meeting all my objectives

I am grateful for...

Today I learned...

How good am I prepared for the next day? 0 25% 50% 75% 100%

- positive thinking = positive preparation = positive outcome -

Main Goals ☐ ☐ ☐

My Big Goal (long-term)

Additional tasks

Exams / tests 1. 2. 3.

Things I need — school supplies ☐ ☐ ☐

People I want to meet — name/reason ☐ ☐ ☐

Today's challenge ☐

My mentor's tasks 1. ☐ 2. ☐

What do I need to do to make this day great?

Today's successes

Incredible ideas

Preparation / learning plan

4:00 pm ☐
5:00 pm ☐
6:00 pm ☐
7:00 pm ☐
8:00 pm ☐
9:00 pm ☐

Efficiency of my 12 hour cycle

hours %

12 3 6 9

How do I evaluate my today's efforts? 0 25% 50% 75% 100%

Reward for meeting all my objectives

I am grateful for...

Today I learned...

How good am I prepared for the next day? 0 25% 50% 75% 100%

"My mind is clear!"

Main Goals ☐ ☐ ☐

My Big Goal (long-term)

Additional tasks

Exams / tests 1. 2. 3.

Things I need — school supplies ☐ ☐ ☐

People I want to meet — name/reason ☐ ☐ ☐

Today's challenge ☐

My mentor's tasks 1. ☐ 2. ☐

What do I need to do to make this day great?

Today's successes

Incredible ideas

Preparation / learning plan

4:00 pm ☐

5:00 pm ☐

6:00 pm ☐

7:00 pm ☐

8:00 pm ☐

9:00 pm ☐

Efficiency of my 12 hour cycle

hours %

12 3 6 9

How do I evaluate my today's efforts? 0 25% 50% 75% 100%

Reward for meeting all my objectives

I am grateful for...

Today I learned...

How good am I prepared for the next day? 0 25% 50% 75% 100%

- identify, describe & control your behavior -

Main Goals ☐ ☐ ☐

My Big Goal (long-term)

Additional tasks

Exams / tests 1. 2. 3.

Things I need — school supplies ☐ ☐ ☐

People I want to meet — name/reason ☐ ☐ ☐

Today's challenge ☐

My mentor's tasks 1. ☐ 2. ☐

What do I need to do to make this day great?

Today's successes

Incredible ideas

Preparation / learning plan

4:00 pm ☐
5:00 pm ☐
6:00 pm ☐
7:00 pm ☐
8:00 pm ☐
9:00 pm ☐

Efficiency of my 12 hour cycle

hours %

12 3 6 9

How do I evaluate my today's efforts? 0 25% 50% 75% 100%

Reward for meeting all my objectives

I am grateful for...

Today I learned...

How good am I prepared for the next day? 0 25% 50% 75% 100%

"Today I will win!"

Main Goals ☐ ☐ ☐

My Big Goal (long-term)

Additional tasks

Exams / tests 1. 2. 3.

Things I need — school supplies ☐ ☐ ☐

People I want to meet — name/reason ☐ ☐ ☐

Today's challenge ☐

My mentor's tasks 1. ☐ 2. ☐

What do I need to do to make this day great?

Today's successes

Incredible ideas

Preparation / learning plan

4:00 pm ☐

5:00 pm ☐

6:00 pm ☐

7:00 pm ☐

8:00 pm ☐

9:00 pm ☐

Efficiency of my 12 hour cycle

hours %

12 3 6 9

How do I evaluate my today's efforts? 0 25% 50% 75% 100%

Reward for meeting all my objectives

I am grateful for...

Today I learned...

How good am I prepared for the next day? 0 25% 50% 75% 100%

Date __/__/____

- success has 3 pillars - ambitions, technique & ethics -

Main Goals ☐ ☐ ☐

My Big Goal (long-term)

Additional tasks

Exams / tests 1. 2. 3.

Things I need — school supplies ☐ ☐ ☐

People I want to meet — name/reason ☐ ☐ ☐

Today's challenge ☐

My mentor's tasks 1. ☐ 2. ☐

What do I need to do to make this day great?

Today's successes

Incredible ideas

Preparation / learning plan

4:00 pm ☐

5:00 pm ☐

6:00 pm ☐

7:00 pm ☐

8:00 pm ☐

9:00 pm ☐

Efficiency of my 12 hour cycle

hours %

12 3 6 9

How do I evaluate my today's efforts? 0 25% 50% 75% 100%

Reward for meeting all my objectives

I am grateful for...

Today I learned...

How good am I prepared for the next day? 0 25% 50% 75% 100%

Date __/__/____

"I determine my results!"

Main Goals ☐ ☐ ☐

My Big Goal (long-term)

Additional tasks

Exams / tests 1. 2. 3.

Things I need — school supplies ☐ ☐ ☐

People I want to meet — name/reason ☐ ☐ ☐

Today's challenge ☐

My mentor's tasks 1. ☐ 2. ☐

What do I need to do to make this day great?

Today's successes

Incredible ideas

Preparation / learning plan

4:00 pm ☐

5:00 pm ☐

6:00 pm ☐

7:00 pm ☐

8:00 pm ☐

9:00 pm ☐

Efficiency of my 12 hour cycle

hours %

12 3 6 9

How do I evaluate my today's efforts? 0 25% 50% 75% 100%

Reward for meeting all my objectives

I am grateful for...

Today I learned...

How good am I prepared for the next day? 0 25% 50% 75% 100%

- to be prepared means to be one step ahead -

Main Goals ☐ ☐ ☐

My Big Goal (long-term)

Additional tasks

Exams / tests 1. 2. 3.

Things I need — school supplies ☐ ☐ ☐

People I want to meet — name/reason ☐ ☐ ☐

Today's challenge ☐

My mentor's tasks 1. ☐ 2. ☐

What do I need to do to make this day great?

Today's successes

Incredible ideas

Preparation / learning plan

4:00 pm ☐

5:00 pm ☐

6:00 pm ☐

7:00 pm ☐

8:00 pm ☐

9:00 pm ☐

Efficiency of my 12 hour cycle

hours %

12 3 6 9

How do I evaluate my today's efforts? 0 25% 50% 75% 100%

Reward for meeting all my objectives

I am grateful for...

Today I learned...

How good am I prepared for the next day? 0 25% 50% 75% 100%

Date __/__/____

"My decisions, my expectations, my success!"

Main Goals ☐ ☐ ☐

My Big Goal (long-term)

Additional tasks

Exams / tests 1. 2. 3.

Things I need — school supplies ☐ ☐ ☐

People I want to meet — name/reason ☐ ☐ ☐

Today's challenge ☐

My mentor's tasks 1. ☐ 2. ☐

What do I need to do to make this day great?

Today's successes

Incredible ideas

Preparation / learning plan

4:00 pm ☐

5:00 pm ☐

6:00 pm ☐

7:00 pm ☐

8:00 pm ☐

9:00 pm ☐

Efficiency of my 12 hour cycle

hours %

12 3 6 9

How do I evaluate my today's efforts? 0 25% 50% 75% 100%

Reward for meeting all my objectives

I am grateful for...

Today I learned...

How good am I prepared for the next day? 0 25% 50% 75% 100%

- learn to control yourself in stressful situations -

Main Goals ☐ ☐ ☐

My Big Goal (long-term)

Additional tasks

Exams / tests 1. 2. 3.

Things I need — school supplies ☐ ☐ ☐

People I want to meet — name/reason ☐ ☐ ☐

Today's challenge ☐

My mentor's tasks 1. ☐ 2. ☐

What do I need to do to make this day great?

Today's successes

Incredible ideas

Preparation / learning plan

4:00 pm ☐
5:00 pm ☐
6:00 pm ☐
7:00 pm ☐
8:00 pm ☐
9:00 pm ☐

Efficiency of my 12 hour cycle

hours %

12
9 3
6

How do I evaluate my today's efforts? 0 25% 50% 75% 100%

Reward for meeting all my objectives

I am grateful for...

Today I learned...

How good am I prepared for the next day? 0 25% 50% 75% 100%

Date __/__/____

"Everyday is a new opportunity!"

Main Goals ☐ ☐ ☐

My Big Goal (long-term)

Additional tasks

Exams / tests 1. 2. 3.

Things I need — school supplies ☐ ☐ ☐

People I want to meet — name/reason ☐ ☐ ☐

Today's challenge ☐

My mentor's tasks 1. ☐ 2. ☐

What do I need to do to make this day great?

Today's successes

Incredible ideas

Preparation / learning plan

4:00 pm ☐

5:00 pm ☐

6:00 pm ☐

7:00 pm ☐

8:00 pm ☐

9:00 pm ☐

Efficiency of my 12 hour cycle

hours %

12 3 6 9

How do I evaluate my today's efforts? 0 25% 50% 75% 100%

Reward for meeting all my objectives

I am grateful for...

Today I learned...

How good am I prepared for the next day? 0 25% 50% 75% 100%

- my best performance = what I'm privileged to acquire -

Main Goals ☐ ☐ ☐

My Big Goal (long-term)

Additional tasks

Exams / tests 1. 2. 3.

Things I need — school supplies ☐ ☐ ☐

People I want to meet — name/reason ☐ ☐ ☐

Today's challenge ☐

My mentor's tasks 1. ☐ 2. ☐

What do I need to do to make this day great?

Today's successes

Incredible ideas

Preparation / learning plan

4:00 pm ☐

5:00 pm ☐

6:00 pm ☐

7:00 pm ☐

8:00 pm ☐

9:00 pm ☐

Efficiency of my 12 hour cycle

hours %

12 3 6 9

How do I evaluate my today's efforts? 0 25% 50% 75% 100%

Reward for meeting all my objectives

I am grateful for...

Today I learned...

How good am I prepared for the next day? 0 25% 50% 75% 100%

Date __ / __ / ____

"Positive toughts = positive results!"

Main Goals ☐ ☐ ☐

My Big Goal (long-term)

Additional tasks

Exams / tests 1. 2. 3.

Things I need — school supplies ☐ ☐ ☐

People I want to meet — name/reason ☐ ☐ ☐

Today's challenge ☐

My mentor's tasks 1. ☐ 2. ☐

What do I need to do to make this day great?

Today's successes

Incredible ideas

Preparation / learning plan

4:00 pm ☐

5:00 pm ☐

6:00 pm ☐

7:00 pm ☐

8:00 pm ☐

9:00 pm ☐

Efficiency of my 12 hour cycle

hours %

12 3 6 9

How do I evaluate my today's efforts? 0 25% 50% 75% 100%

Reward for meeting all my objectives

I am grateful for...

Today I learned...

How good am I prepared for the next day? 0 25% 50% 75% 100%

- strong mind shell protects us from external stirs -

Main Goals ☐ ☐ ☐

My Big Goal (long-term)

Additional tasks

Exams / tests 1. 2. 3.

Things I need — school supplies ☐ ☐ ☐

People I want to meet — name/reason ☐ ☐ ☐

Today's challenge ☐

My mentor's tasks 1. ☐ 2. ☐

What do I need to do to make this day great?

Today's successes

Incredible ideas

Preparation / learning plan

4:00 pm ☐
5:00 pm ☐
6:00 pm ☐
7:00 pm ☐
8:00 pm ☐
9:00 pm ☐

Efficiency of my 12 hour cycle

hours %

12 3 6 9

How do I evaluate my today's efforts? 0 25% 50% 75% 100%

Reward for meeting all my objectives

I am grateful for...

Today I learned...

How good am I prepared for the next day? 0 25% 50% 75% 100%

Date __/__/____

"Today I will use my full potential!"

Main Goals ☐ ☐ ☐

My Big Goal (long-term)

Additional tasks

Exams / tests 1. 2. 3.

Things I need — school supplies ☐ ☐ ☐

People I want to meet — name/reason ☐ ☐ ☐

Today's challenge ☐

My mentor's tasks 1. ☐ 2. ☐

What do I need to do to make this day great?

Today's successes

Incredible ideas

Preparation / learning plan

4:00 pm ☐

5:00 pm ☐

6:00 pm ☐

7:00 pm ☐

8:00 pm ☐

9:00 pm ☐

Efficiency of my 12 hour cycle

hours %

12 3 6 9

How do I evaluate my today's efforts? 0 25% 50% 75% 100%

Reward for meeting all my objectives

I am grateful for...

Today I learned...

How good am I prepared for the next day? 0 25% 50% 75% 100%

- always think on the actual moment only -

Main Goals ☐ ☐ ☐

My Big Goal (long-term)

Additional tasks

Exams / tests 1. 2. 3.

Things I need — school supplies ☐ ☐ ☐

People I want to meet — name/reason ☐ ☐ ☐

Today's challenge ☐

My mentor's tasks 1. ☐ 2. ☐

What do I need to do to make this day great?

Today's successes

Incredible ideas

Preparation / learning plan

4:00 pm ☐
5:00 pm ☐
6:00 pm ☐
7:00 pm ☐
8:00 pm ☐
9:00 pm ☐

Efficiency of my 12 hour cycle

hours %

12 3 6 9

How do I evaluate my today's efforts? 0 25% 50% 75% 100%

Reward for meeting all my objectives

I am grateful for...

Today I learned...

How good am I prepared for the next day? 0 25% 50% 75% 100%

Date __/__/____ ____________

"I'm the Power! I'm the Control! I'm the Victory!"

Main Goals ☐ ☐ ☐

My Big Goal (long-term)

Additional tasks

Exams / tests 1. 2. 3.

Things I need — school supplies ☐ ☐ ☐

People I want to meet — name/reason ☐ ☐ ☐

Today's challenge ☐

My mentor's tasks 1. ☐ 2. ☐

What do I need to do to make this day great?

Today's successes

Incredible ideas

Preparation / learning plan

4:00 pm ☐

5:00 pm ☐

6:00 pm ☐

7:00 pm ☐

8:00 pm ☐

9:00 pm ☐

Efficiency of my 12 hour cycle: hours %

12 3 6 9

How do I evaluate my today's efforts? 0 25% 50% 75% 100%

Reward for meeting all my objectives

I am grateful for...

Today I learned...

How good am I prepared for the next day? 0 25% 50% 75% 100%

- your opportunity, your trophy is waiting for you -

Main Goals ☐ ☐ ☐

My Big Goal (long-term)

Additional tasks

Exams / tests 1. 2. 3.

Things I need — school supplies ☐ ☐ ☐

People I want to meet — name/reason ☐ ☐ ☐

Today's challenge ☐

My mentor's tasks 1. ☐ 2. ☐

What do I need to do to make this day great?

Today's successes

Incredible ideas

Preparation / learning plan

4:00 pm ☐

5:00 pm ☐

6:00 pm ☐

7:00 pm ☐

8:00 pm ☐

9:00 pm ☐

Efficiency of my 12 hour cycle

hours %

12 3 6 9

How do I evaluate my today's efforts? 0 25% 50% 75% 100%

Reward for meeting all my objectives

I am grateful for...

Today I learned...

How good am I prepared for the next day? 0 25% 50% 75% 100%

"I'm creating!"

Main Goals ☐ ☐ ☐

My Big Goal (long-term)

Additional tasks

Exams / tests 1. 2. 3.

Things I need — school supplies ☐ ☐ ☐

People I want to meet — name/reason ☐ ☐ ☐

Today's challenge ☐

My mentor's tasks 1. ☐ 2. ☐

What do I need to do to make this day great?

Today's successes

Incredible ideas

Preparation / learning plan

4:00 pm ☐
5:00 pm ☐
6:00 pm ☐
7:00 pm ☐
8:00 pm ☐
9:00 pm ☐

Efficiency of my 12 hour cycle
hours %

12 3 6 9

How do I evaluate my today's efforts? 0 25% 50% 75% 100%

Reward for meeting all my objectives

I am grateful for...

Today I learned...

How good am I prepared for the next day? 0 25% 50% 75% 100%

- bomb yourself with positive thoughts & energy -

Main Goals ☐ ☐ ☐

My Big Goal (long-term)

Additional tasks

Exams / tests 1. 2. 3.

Things I need — school supplies ☐ ☐ ☐

People I want to meet — name/reason ☐ ☐ ☐

Today's challenge ☐

My mentor's tasks 1. ☐ 2. ☐

What do I need to do to make this day great?

Today's successes

Incredible ideas

Preparation / learning plan

4:00 pm ☐

5:00 pm ☐

6:00 pm ☐

7:00 pm ☐

8:00 pm ☐

9:00 pm ☐

Efficiency of my 12 hour cycle

hours %

12 3 6 9

How do I evaluate my today's efforts? 0 25% 50% 75% 100%

Reward for meeting all my objectives

I am grateful for...

Today I learned...

How good am I prepared for the next day? 0 25% 50% 75% 100%

Date __/__/____

"I'm reaching!"

Main Goals ☐ ☐ ☐

My Big Goal (long-term)

Additional tasks

Exams / tests 1. 2. 3.

Things I need — school supplies ☐ ☐ ☐

People I want to meet — name/reason ☐ ☐ ☐

Today's challenge ☐

My mentor's tasks 1. ☐ 2. ☐

What do I need to do to make this day great?

Today's successes

Incredible ideas

Preparation / learning plan

4:00 pm ☐

5:00 pm ☐

6:00 pm ☐

7:00 pm ☐

8:00 pm ☐

9:00 pm ☐

Efficiency of my 12 hour cycle

hours %

12 3 6 9

How do I evaluate my today's efforts? 0 25% 50% 75% 100%

Reward for meeting all my objectives

I am grateful for...

Today I learned...

How good am I prepared for the next day? 0 25% 50% 75% 100%

- mental relax = physical relax -

Main Goals ☐ ☐ ☐

My Big Goal (long-term)

Additional tasks

Exams / tests 1. 2. 3.

Things I need — school supplies ☐ ☐ ☐

People I want to meet — name/reason ☐ ☐ ☐

Today's challenge ☐

My mentor's tasks 1. ☐ 2. ☐

What do I need to do to make this day great?

Today's successes

Incredible ideas

Preparation / learning plan

4:00 pm ☐

5:00 pm ☐

6:00 pm ☐

7:00 pm ☐

8:00 pm ☐

9:00 pm ☐

Efficiency of my 12 hour cycle

hours %

12 3 6 9

How do I evaluate my today's efforts? 0 25% 50% 75% 100%

Reward for meeting all my objectives

I am grateful for...

Today I learned...

How good am I prepared for the next day? 0 25% 50% 75% 100%

"I'm creating my future!"

Main Goals ☐ ☐ ☐

My Big Goal (long-term)

Additional tasks

Exams / tests 1. 2. 3.

Things I need — school supplies ☐ ☐ ☐

People I want to meet — name/reason ☐ ☐ ☐

Today's challenge ☐

My mentor's tasks 1. ☐ 2. ☐

What do I need to do to make this day great?

Today's successes

Incredible ideas

Preparation / learning plan

4:00 pm ☐

5:00 pm ☐

6:00 pm ☐

7:00 pm ☐

8:00 pm ☐

9:00 pm ☐

Efficiency of my 12 hour cycle

hours %

12 3 6 9

How do I evaluate my today's efforts? 0 25% 50% 75% 100%

Reward for meeting all my objectives

I am grateful for...

Today I learned...

How good am I prepared for the next day? 0 25% 50% 75% 100%

- you will have better results than before -

Main Goals ☐ ☐ ☐

My Big Goal (long-term)

Additional tasks

Exams / tests 1. 2. 3.

Things I need — school supplies ☐ ☐ ☐

People I want to meet — name/reason ☐ ☐ ☐

Today's challenge ☐

My mentor's tasks 1. ☐ 2. ☐

What do I need to do to make this day great?

Today's successes

Incredible ideas

Preparation / learning plan

4:00 pm ☐
5:00 pm ☐
6:00 pm ☐
7:00 pm ☐
8:00 pm ☐
9:00 pm ☐

Efficiency of my 12 hour cycle

hours %

12 3 6 9

How do I evaluate my today's efforts? 0 25% 50% 75% 100%

Reward for meeting all my objectives

I am grateful for...

Today I learned...

How good am I prepared for the next day? 0 25% 50% 75% 100%

Date __/__/____

"I am the Star!"

Main Goals ☐ ☐ ☐

My Big Goal (long-term)

Additional tasks

Exams / tests 1. 2. 3.

Things I need — school supplies ☐ ☐ ☐

People I want to meet — name/reason ☐ ☐ ☐

Today's challenge ☐

My mentor's tasks 1. ☐ 2. ☐

What do I need to do to make this day great?

Today's successes

Incredible ideas

Preparation / learning plan

4:00 pm ☐

5:00 pm ☐

6:00 pm ☐

7:00 pm ☐

8:00 pm ☐

9:00 pm ☐

Efficiency of my 12 hour cycle

hours %

12 3 6 9

How do I evaluate my today's efforts? 0 25% 50% 75% 100%

Reward for meeting all my objectives

I am grateful for...

Today I learned...

How good am I prepared for the next day? 0 25% 50% 75% 100%

- result = preparation + evaluation of my possibilities -

Main Goals ☐ ☐ ☐

My Big Goal (long-term)

Additional tasks

Exams / tests 1. 2. 3.

Things I need — school supplies ☐ ☐ ☐

People I want to meet — name/reason ☐ ☐ ☐

Today's challenge ☐

My mentor's tasks 1. ☐ 2. ☐

What do I need to do to make this day great?

Today's successes

Incredible ideas

Preparation / learning plan

4:00 pm ☐
5:00 pm ☐
6:00 pm ☐
7:00 pm ☐
8:00 pm ☐
9:00 pm ☐

Efficiency of my 12 hour cycle

hours %

12 3 6 9

How do I evaluate my today's efforts? 0 25% 50% 75% 100%

Reward for meeting all my objectives

I am grateful for...

Today I learned...

How good am I prepared for the next day? 0 25% 50% 75% 100%

"I believe in my preparation and in my abilities!"

Main Goals ☐ ☐ ☐

My Big Goal (long-term)

Additional tasks

Exams / tests 1. 2. 3.

Things I need — school supplies ☐ ☐ ☐

People I want to meet — name/reason ☐ ☐ ☐

Today's challenge ☐

My mentor's tasks 1. ☐ 2. ☐

What do I need to do to make this day great?

Today's successes

Incredible ideas

Preparation / learning plan

4:00 pm ☐
5:00 pm ☐
6:00 pm ☐
7:00 pm ☐
8:00 pm ☐
9:00 pm ☐

Efficiency of my 12 hour cycle
hours %

12 3 6 9

How do I evaluate my today's efforts? 0 25% 50% 75% 100%

Reward for meeting all my objectives

I am grateful for...

Today I learned...

How good am I prepared for the next day? 0 25% 50% 75% 100%

- examine the situation realistically -

Main Goals ☐ ☐ ☐

My Big Goal (long-term)

Additional tasks

Exams / tests 1. 2. 3.

Things I need — school supplies ☐ ☐ ☐

People I want to meet — name/reason ☐ ☐ ☐

Today's challenge ☐

My mentor's tasks 1. ☐ 2. ☐

What do I need to do to make this day great?

Today's successes

Incredible ideas

Preparation / learning plan

4:00 pm ☐

5:00 pm ☐

6:00 pm ☐

7:00 pm ☐

8:00 pm ☐

9:00 pm ☐

Efficiency of my 12 hour cycle

hours %

12 3 6 9

How do I evaluate my today's efforts? 0 25% 50% 75% 100%

Reward for meeting all my objectives

I am grateful for...

Today I learned...

How good am I prepared for the next day? 0 25% 50% 75% 100%

Date __/__/____

"Today will be unbelievable!"

Main Goals ☐ ☐ ☐

My Big Goal (long-term)

Additional tasks

Exams / tests 1. 2. 3.

Things I need — school supplies ☐ ☐ ☐

People I want to meet — name/reason ☐ ☐ ☐

Today's challenge ☐

My mentor's tasks 1. ☐ 2. ☐

What do I need to do to make this day great?

Today's successes

Incredible ideas

Preparation / learning plan

4:00 pm ☐

5:00 pm ☐

6:00 pm ☐

7:00 pm ☐

8:00 pm ☐

9:00 pm ☐

Efficiency of my 12 hour cycle

hours %

12 3 6 9

How do I evaluate my today's efforts? 0 25% 50% 75% 100%

Reward for meeting all my objectives

I am grateful for...

Today I learned...

How good am I prepared for the next day? 0 25% 50% 75% 100%

- you don't want to run away -

Main Goals ☐ ☐ ☐

My Big Goal (long-term)

Additional tasks

Exams / tests 1. 2. 3.

Things I need — school supplies ☐ ☐ ☐

People I want to meet — name/reason ☐ ☐ ☐

Today's challenge ☐

My mentor's tasks 1. ☐ 2. ☐

What do I need to do to make this day great?

Today's successes

Incredible ideas

Preparation / learning plan

4:00 pm ☐

5:00 pm ☐

6:00 pm ☐

7:00 pm ☐

8:00 pm ☐

9:00 pm ☐

Efficiency of my 12 hour cycle

hours %

12 3 6 9

How do I evaluate my today's efforts? 0 25% 50% 75% 100%

Reward for meeting all my objectives

I am grateful for...

Today I learned...

How good am I prepared for the next day? 0 25% 50% 75% 100%

"I will make my day!"

Main Goals ☐ ☐ ☐

My Big Goal (long-term)

Additional tasks

Exams / tests 1. 2. 3.

Things I need — school supplies ☐ ☐ ☐

People I want to meet — name/reason ☐ ☐ ☐

Today's challenge ☐

My mentor's tasks 1. ☐ 2. ☐

What do I need to do to make this day great?

Today's successes

Incredible ideas

Preparation / learning plan

4:00 pm ☐
5:00 pm ☐
6:00 pm ☐
7:00 pm ☐
8:00 pm ☐
9:00 pm ☐

Efficiency of my 12 hour cycle

hours %

12 3 6 9

How do I evaluate my today's efforts? 0 25% 50% 75% 100%

Reward for meeting all my objectives

I am grateful for...

Today I learned...

How good am I prepared for the next day? 0 25% 50% 75% 100%

- you want to understand it -

Main Goals ☐ ☐ ☐

My Big Goal (long-term)

Additional tasks

Exams / tests 1. 2. 3.

Things I need — school supplies ☐ ☐ ☐

People I want to meet — name/reason ☐ ☐ ☐

Today's challenge ☐

My mentor's tasks 1. ☐ 2. ☐

What do I need to do to make this day great?

Today's successes

Incredible ideas

Preparation / learning plan

4:00 pm ☐
5:00 pm ☐
6:00 pm ☐
7:00 pm ☐
8:00 pm ☐
9:00 pm ☐

Efficiency of my 12 hour cycle

hours %

12 3 6 9

How do I evaluate my today's efforts? 0 25% 50% 75% 100%

Reward for meeting all my objectives

I am grateful for...

Today I learned...

How good am I prepared for the next day? 0 25% 50% 75% 100%

"The opportunity is in my hands!"

Main Goals ☐ ☐ ☐

My Big Goal (long-term)

Additional tasks

Exams / tests 1. 2. 3.

Things I need — school supplies ☐ ☐ ☐

People I want to meet — name/reason ☐ ☐ ☐

Today's challenge ☐

My mentor's tasks 1. ☐ 2. ☐

What do I need to do to make this day great?

Today's successes

Incredible ideas

Preparation / learning plan

4:00 pm ☐

5:00 pm ☐

6:00 pm ☐

7:00 pm ☐

8:00 pm ☐

9:00 pm ☐

Efficiency of my 12 hour cycle

hours %

12 3 6 9

How do I evaluate my today's efforts? 0 25% 50% 75% 100%

Reward for meeting all my objectives

I am grateful for...

Today I learned...

How good am I prepared for the next day? 0 25% 50% 75% 100%

- you want to control it -

Main Goals ☐ ☐ ☐

My Big Goal (long-term)

Additional tasks

Exams / tests 1. 2. 3.

Things I need — school supplies ☐ ☐ ☐

People I want to meet — name/reason ☐ ☐ ☐

Today's challenge ☐

My mentor's tasks 1. ☐ 2. ☐

What do I need to do to make this day great?

Today's successes

Incredible ideas

Preparation / learning plan

4:00 pm ☐
5:00 pm ☐
6:00 pm ☐
7:00 pm ☐
8:00 pm ☐
9:00 pm ☐

Efficiency of my 12 hour cycle

hours %

12 3 6 9

How do I evaluate my today's efforts? 0 25% 50% 75% 100%

Reward for meeting all my objectives

I am grateful for...

Today I learned...

How good am I prepared for the next day? 0 25% 50% 75% 100%

Date __/__/____

"My success is created by my actions!"

Main Goals ☐ ☐ ☐

My Big Goal (long-term)

Additional tasks

Exams / tests 1. 2. 3.

Things I need — school supplies ☐ ☐ ☐

People I want to meet — name/reason ☐ ☐ ☐

Today's challenge ☐

My mentor's tasks 1. ☐ 2. ☐

What do I need to do to make this day great?

Today's successes

Incredible ideas

Preparation / learning plan

4:00 pm ☐

5:00 pm ☐

6:00 pm ☐

7:00 pm ☐

8:00 pm ☐

9:00 pm ☐

Efficiency of my 12 hour cycle

hours %

12 3 6 9

How do I evaluate my today's efforts? 0 25% 50% 75% 100%

Reward for meeting all my objectives

I am grateful for...

Today I learned...

How good am I prepared for the next day? 0 25% 50% 75% 100%

- you want to win -

Main Goals ☐ ☐ ☐

My Big Goal (long-term)

Additional tasks

Exams / tests 1. 2. 3.

Things I need — school supplies ☐ ☐ ☐

People I want to meet — name/reason ☐ ☐ ☐

Today's challenge ☐

My mentor's tasks 1. ☐ 2. ☐

What do I need to do to make this day great?

Today's successes

Incredible ideas

Preparation / learning plan

4:00 pm ☐

5:00 pm ☐

6:00 pm ☐

7:00 pm ☐

8:00 pm ☐

9:00 pm ☐

Efficiency of my 12 hour cycle

hours %

12 3 6 9

How do I evaluate my today's efforts? 0 25% 50% 75% 100%

Reward for meeting all my objectives

I am grateful for...

Today I learned...

How good am I prepared for the next day? 0 25% 50% 75% 100%

Date __ / __ / ____

"What competition?"

Main Goals ☐ ☐ ☐

My Big Goal (long-term)

Additional tasks

Exams / tests 1. 2. 3.

Things I need — school supplies ☐ ☐ ☐

People I want to meet — name/reason ☐ ☐ ☐

Today's challenge ☐

My mentor's tasks 1. ☐ 2. ☐

What do I need to do to make this day great?

Today's successes

Incredible ideas

Preparation / learning plan

4:00 pm ☐

5:00 pm ☐

6:00 pm ☐

7:00 pm ☐

8:00 pm ☐

9:00 pm ☐

Efficiency of my 12 hour cycle

hours %

12 3 6 9

How do I evaluate my today's efforts? 0 25% 50% 75% 100%

Reward for meeting all my objectives

I am grateful for...

Today I learned...

How good am I prepared for the next day? 0 25% 50% 75% 100%

- customize your potential and determine your results -

Main Goals ☐ ☐ ☐

My Big Goal (long-term)

Additional tasks

Exams / tests 1. 2. 3.

Things I need — school supplies ☐ ☐ ☐

People I want to meet — name/reason ☐ ☐ ☐

Today's challenge ☐

My mentor's tasks 1. ☐ 2. ☐

What do I need to do to make this day great?

Today's successes

Incredible ideas

Preparation / learning plan

4:00 pm ☐

5:00 pm ☐

6:00 pm ☐

7:00 pm ☐

8:00 pm ☐

9:00 pm ☐

Efficiency of my 12 hour cycle

hours %

12 3 6 9

How do I evaluate my today's efforts? 0 25% 50% 75% 100%

Reward for meeting all my objectives

I am grateful for...

Today I learned...

How good am I prepared for the next day? 0 25% 50% 75% 100%

Date __/__/____ ____________

"I control my internal balance!"

Main Goals ☐ ☐ ☐

My Big Goal (long-term)

Additional tasks

Exams / tests 1. ____ 2. ____ 3. ____

Things I need — school supplies ☐ ☐ ☐

People I want to meet — name/reason ☐ ☐ ☐

Today's challenge ☐

My mentor's tasks 1. ____ ☐ 2. ____ ☐

What do I need to do to make this day great?

Today's successes

Incredible ideas

Preparation / learning plan

4:00 pm ☐

5:00 pm ☐

6:00 pm ☐

7:00 pm ☐

8:00 pm ☐

9:00 pm ☐

Efficiency of my 12 hour cycle

____ hours ____ %

12 3 6 9

How do I evaluate my today's efforts? 0 25% 50% 75% 100%

Reward for meeting all my objectives

I am grateful for...

Today I learned...

How good am I prepared for the next day? 0 25% 50% 75% 100%

Date __/__/____

- balance your energy -

Main Goals ☐ ☐ ☐

My Big Goal (long-term)

Additional tasks

Exams / tests 1. 2. 3.

Things I need — school supplies ☐ ☐ ☐

People I want to meet — name/reason ☐ ☐ ☐

Today's challenge ☐

My mentor's tasks 1. ☐ 2. ☐

What do I need to do to make this day great?

Today's successes

Incredible ideas

Preparation / learning plan

4:00 pm ☐

5:00 pm ☐

6:00 pm ☐

7:00 pm ☐

8:00 pm ☐

9:00 pm ☐

Efficiency of my 12 hour cycle

hours %

12 3 6 9

How do I evaluate my today's efforts? 0 25% 50% 75% 100%

Reward for meeting all my objectives

I am grateful for...

Today I learned...

How good am I prepared for the next day? 0 25% 50% 75% 100%

Date __ / __ / ____ __________

"I'm creating the picture of my Tomorrow!"

Main Goals ☐ ☐ ☐

My Big Goal (long-term)

Additional tasks

Exams / tests 1. ______ 2. ______ 3. ______

Things I need — school supplies ☐ ☐ ☐

People I want to meet — name/reason ☐ ☐ ☐

Today's challenge ☐

My mentor's tasks 1. ______ ☐ 2. ______ ☐

What do I need to do to make this day great?

Today's successes

Incredible ideas

Preparation / learning plan

4:00 pm ☐

5:00 pm ☐

6:00 pm ☐

7:00 pm ☐

8:00 pm ☐

9:00 pm ☐

Efficiency of my 12 hour cycle

hours %

12 3 6 9

How do I evaluate my today's efforts? 0 25% 50% 75% 100%

Reward for meeting all my objectives

I am grateful for...

Today I learned...

How good am I prepared for the next day? 0 25% 50% 75% 100%

- you must categorize the informations in the learning material -

Main Goals ☐ ☐ ☐

My Big Goal (long-term)

Additional tasks

Exams / tests 1. 2. 3.

Things I need — school supplies ☐ ☐ ☐

People I want to meet — name/reason ☐ ☐ ☐

Today's challenge ☐

My mentor's tasks 1. ☐ 2. ☐

What do I need to do to make this day great?

Today's successes

Incredible ideas

Preparation / learning plan

4:00 pm ☐
5:00 pm ☐
6:00 pm ☐
7:00 pm ☐
8:00 pm ☐
9:00 pm ☐

Efficiency of my 12 hour cycle

hours %

12 3 6 9

How do I evaluate my today's efforts? 0 25% 50% 75% 100%

Reward for meeting all my objectives

I am grateful for...

Today I learned...

How good am I prepared for the next day? 0 25% 50% 75% 100%

"I'll do my best!"

Main Goals ☐ ☐ ☐

My Big Goal (long-term)

Additional tasks

Exams / tests 1. 2. 3.

Things I need — school supplies ☐ ☐ ☐

People I want to meet — name/reason ☐ ☐ ☐

Today's challenge ☐

My mentor's tasks 1. ☐ 2. ☐

What do I need to do to make this day great?

Today's successes

Incredible ideas

Preparation / learning plan

4:00 pm ☐

5:00 pm ☐

6:00 pm ☐

7:00 pm ☐

8:00 pm ☐

9:00 pm ☐

Efficiency of my 12 hour cycle

hours %

12 3 6 9

How do I evaluate my today's efforts? 0 25% 50% 75% 100%

Reward for meeting all my objectives

I am grateful for...

Today I learned...

How good am I prepared for the next day? 0 25% 50% 75% 100%

- being unprepared = gambling with your potential -

Main Goals ☐ ☐ ☐

My Big Goal (long-term)

Additional tasks

Exams / tests 1. 2. 3.

Things I need — school supplies ☐ ☐ ☐

People I want to meet — name/reason ☐ ☐ ☐

Today's challenge ☐

My mentor's tasks 1. ☐ 2. ☐

What do I need to do to make this day great?

Today's successes

Incredible ideas

Preparation / learning plan

4:00 pm ☐
5:00 pm ☐
6:00 pm ☐
7:00 pm ☐
8:00 pm ☐
9:00 pm ☐

Efficiency of my 12 hour cycle

hours %

12 3 6 9

How do I evaluate my today's efforts? 0 25% 50% 75% 100%

Reward for meeting all my objectives

I am grateful for...

Today I learned...

How good am I prepared for the next day? 0 25% 50% 75% 100%

"Step by step I'm closer to my goals!"

Main Goals ☐ ☐ ☐

My Big Goal (long-term)

Additional tasks

Exams / tests 1. 2. 3.

Things I need — school supplies ☐ ☐ ☐

People I want to meet — name/reason ☐ ☐ ☐

Today's challenge ☐

My mentor's tasks 1. ☐ 2. ☐

What do I need to do to make this day great?

Today's successes

Incredible ideas

Preparation / learning plan

4:00 pm ☐

5:00 pm ☐

6:00 pm ☐

7:00 pm ☐

8:00 pm ☐

9:00 pm ☐

Efficiency of my 12 hour cycle

hours %

12 3 6 9

How do I evaluate my today's efforts? 0 25% 50% 75% 100%

Reward for meeting all my objectives

I am grateful for...

Today I learned...

How good am I prepared for the next day? 0 25% 50% 75% 100%

- you need patience and clear goal -

Main Goals ☐ ☐ ☐

My Big Goal (long-term)

Additional tasks

Exams / tests 1. 2. 3.

Things I need — school supplies ☐ ☐ ☐

People I want to meet — name/reason ☐ ☐ ☐

Today's challenge ☐

My mentor's tasks 1. ☐ 2. ☐

What do I need to do to make this day great?

Today's successes

Incredible ideas

Preparation / learning plan

4:00 pm ☐

5:00 pm ☐

6:00 pm ☐

7:00 pm ☐

8:00 pm ☐

9:00 pm ☐

Efficiency of my 12 hour cycle

hours %

12 3 6 9

How do I evaluate my today's efforts? 0 25% 50% 75% 100%

Reward for meeting all my objectives

I am grateful for...

Today I learned...

How good am I prepared for the next day? 0 25% 50% 75% 100%

Date __ / __ / ____ __________

"Reaching the goals is my new standard!"

Main Goals ☐ ☐ ☐

My Big Goal (long-term)

Additional tasks

Exams / tests 1. 2. 3.

Things I need — school supplies ☐ ☐ ☐

People I want to meet — name/reason ☐ ☐ ☐

Today's challenge ☐

My mentor's tasks 1. ☐ 2. ☐

What do I need to do to make this day great?

Today's successes

Incredible ideas

Preparation / learning plan

4:00 pm ☐

5:00 pm ☐

6:00 pm ☐

7:00 pm ☐

8:00 pm ☐

9:00 pm ☐

Efficiency of my 12 hour cycle

hours %

12 3 6 9

How do I evaluate my today's efforts? 0 25% 50% 75% 100%

Reward for meeting all my objectives

I am grateful for...

Today I learned...

How good am I prepared for the next day? 0 25% 50% 75% 100%

- setting up the priorities is the 1st step to the change -

Main Goals ☐ ☐ ☐

My Big Goal (long-term)

Additional tasks

Exams / tests 1. 2. 3.

Things I need — school supplies ☐ ☐ ☐

People I want to meet — name/reason ☐ ☐ ☐

Today's challenge ☐

My mentor's tasks 1. ☐ 2. ☐

What do I need to do to make this day great?

Today's successes

Incredible ideas

Preparation / learning plan

4:00 pm ☐
5:00 pm ☐
6:00 pm ☐
7:00 pm ☐
8:00 pm ☐
9:00 pm ☐

Efficiency of my 12 hour cycle

hours %

12 3 6 9

How do I evaluate my today's efforts? 0 25% 50% 75% 100%

Reward for meeting all my objectives

I am grateful for...

Today I learned...

How good am I prepared for the next day? 0 25% 50% 75% 100%

"I'm patient and humble!"

Main Goals ☐ ☐ ☐

My Big Goal (long-term)

Additional tasks

Exams / tests 1. 2. 3.

Things I need — school supplies ☐ ☐ ☐

People I want to meet — name/reason ☐ ☐ ☐

Today's challenge ☐

My mentor's tasks 1. ☐ 2. ☐

What do I need to do to make this day great?

Today's successes

Incredible ideas

Preparation / learning plan

4:00 pm ☐
5:00 pm ☐
6:00 pm ☐
7:00 pm ☐
8:00 pm ☐
9:00 pm ☐

Efficiency of my 12 hour cycle

hours %

12 3 6 9

How do I evaluate my today's efforts? 0 25% 50% 75% 100%

Reward for meeting all my objectives

I am grateful for...

Today I learned...

How good am I prepared for the next day? 0 25% 50% 75% 100%

- create a wise plan for desired level of efficiency -

Main Goals ☐ ☐ ☐

My Big Goal (long-term)

Additional tasks

Exams / tests 1. 2. 3.

Things I need — school supplies ☐ ☐ ☐

People I want to meet — name/reason ☐ ☐ ☐

Today's challenge ☐

My mentor's tasks 1. ☐ 2. ☐

What do I need to do to make this day great?

Today's successes

Incredible ideas

Preparation / learning plan

4:00 pm ☐

5:00 pm ☐

6:00 pm ☐

7:00 pm ☐

8:00 pm ☐

9:00 pm ☐

Efficiency of my 12 hour cycle

hours %

12 3 6 9

How do I evaluate my today's efforts? 0 25% 50% 75% 100%

Reward for meeting all my objectives

I am grateful for...

Today I learned...

How good am I prepared for the next day? 0 25% 50% 75% 100%

Date __/__/____ ____________

"All I need for beginning is 1 positive thought!"

Main Goals ☐ ☐ ☐

My Big Goal (long-term)

Additional tasks

Exams / tests 1. ______ 2. ______ 3. ______

Things I need — school supplies ☐ ☐ ☐

People I want to meet — name/reason ☐ ☐ ☐

Today's challenge ☐

My mentor's tasks 1. ______ ☐ 2. ______ ☐

What do I need to do to make this day great?

Today's successes

Incredible ideas

Preparation / learning plan

4:00 pm ☐

5:00 pm ☐

6:00 pm ☐

7:00 pm ☐

8:00 pm ☐

9:00 pm ☐

Efficiency of my 12 hour cycle

hours %

12 3 6 9

How do I evaluate my today's efforts? 0 25% 50% 75% 100%

Reward for meeting all my objectives

I am grateful for...

Today I learned...

How good am I prepared for the next day? 0 25% 50% 75% 100%

- examine your daily activities in every detail -

Main Goals ☐ ☐ ☐

My Big Goal (long-term)

Additional tasks

Exams / tests 1. 2. 3.

Things I need — school supplies ☐ ☐ ☐

People I want to meet — name/reason ☐ ☐ ☐

Today's challenge ☐

My mentor's tasks 1. ☐ 2. ☐

What do I need to do to make this day great?

Today's successes

Incredible ideas

Preparation / learning plan

4:00 pm ☐

5:00 pm ☐

6:00 pm ☐

7:00 pm ☐

8:00 pm ☐

9:00 pm ☐

Efficiency of my 12 hour cycle

hours %

12 3 6 9

How do I evaluate my today's efforts? 0 25% 50% 75% 100%

Reward for meeting all my objectives

I am grateful for...

Today I learned...

How good am I prepared for the next day? 0 25% 50% 75% 100%

Date __/__/____ LEO - Learning organizer

"Today will be better than yesterday!"

Main Goals ☐ ☐ ☐

My Big Goal (long-term)

Additional tasks

Exams / tests 1. 2. 3.

Things I need — school supplies ☐ ☐ ☐

People I want to meet — name/reason ☐ ☐ ☐

Today's challenge ☐

My mentor's tasks 1. ☐ 2. ☐

What do I need to do to make this day great?

Today's successes

Incredible ideas

Preparation / learning plan

4:00 pm ☐

5:00 pm ☐

6:00 pm ☐

7:00 pm ☐

8:00 pm ☐

9:00 pm ☐

Efficiency of my 12 hour cycle

hours %

12 3 6 9

How do I evaluate my today's efforts? 0 25% 50% 75% 100%

Reward for meeting all my objectives

I am grateful for...

Today I learned...

How good am I prepared for the next day? 0 25% 50% 75% 100%

- categorize the learning material by colors, shapes, etc. -

Main Goals ☐ ☐ ☐

My Big Goal (long-term)

Additional tasks

Exams / tests 1. ______ 2. ______ 3. ______

Things I need — school supplies ☐ ☐ ☐

People I want to meet — name/reason ☐ ☐ ☐

Today's challenge ☐

My mentor's tasks 1. ______ ☐ 2. ______ ☐

What do I need to do to make this day great?

Today's successes

Incredible ideas

Preparation / learning plan

4:00 pm ☐

5:00 pm ☐

6:00 pm ☐

7:00 pm ☐

8:00 pm ☐

9:00 pm ☐

Efficiency of my 12 hour cycle

[ ] hours [ ] %

12 3 6 9

How do I evaluate my today's efforts? 0 25% 50% 75% 100%

Reward for meeting all my objectives

I am grateful for...

Today I learned...

How good am I prepared for the next day? 0 25% 50% 75% 100%

Date __/__/____

"The Secret to my success is the correct Strategy!"

Main Goals ☐ ☐ ☐

My Big Goal (long-term)

Additional tasks

Exams / tests 1. 2. 3.

Things I need — school supplies ☐ ☐ ☐

People I want to meet — name/reason ☐ ☐ ☐

Today's challenge ☐

My mentor's tasks 1. ☐ 2. ☐

What do I need to do to make this day great?

Today's successes

Incredible ideas

Preparation / learning plan

4:00 pm ☐

5:00 pm ☐

6:00 pm ☐

7:00 pm ☐

8:00 pm ☐

9:00 pm ☐

Efficiency of my 12 hour cycle

hours %

12 3 6 9

How do I evaluate my today's efforts? 0 25% 50% 75% 100%

Reward for meeting all my objectives

I am grateful for...

Today I learned...

How good am I prepared for the next day? 0 25% 50% 75% 100%

- know weak and strong aspects of your personality -

Main Goals ☐ ☐ ☐

My Big Goal (long-term)

Additional tasks

Exams / tests 1. 2. 3.

Things I need — school supplies ☐ ☐ ☐

People I want to meet — name/reason ☐ ☐ ☐

Today's challenge ☐

My mentor's tasks 1. ☐ 2. ☐

What do I need to do to make this day great?

Today's successes

Incredible ideas

Preparation / learning plan

4:00 pm ☐

5:00 pm ☐

6:00 pm ☐

7:00 pm ☐

8:00 pm ☐

9:00 pm ☐

Efficiency of my 12 hour cycle

hours %

12 3 6 9

How do I evaluate my today's efforts? 0 25% 50% 75% 100%

Reward for meeting all my objectives

I am grateful for...

Today I learned...

How good am I prepared for the next day? 0 25% 50% 75% 100%

"Self-confidence, activity and commitment!"

Main Goals ☐ ☐ ☐

My Big Goal (long-term)

Additional tasks

Exams / tests 1. 2. 3.

Things I need — school supplies ☐ ☐ ☐

People I want to meet — name/reason ☐ ☐ ☐

Today's challenge ☐

My mentor's tasks 1. ☐ 2. ☐

What do I need to do to make this day great?

Today's successes

Incredible ideas

Preparation / learning plan

4:00 pm ☐

5:00 pm ☐

6:00 pm ☐

7:00 pm ☐

8:00 pm ☐

9:00 pm ☐

Efficiency of my 12 hour cycle

hours %

12 3 6 9

How do I evaluate my today's efforts? 0 25% 50% 75% 100%

Reward for meeting all my objectives

I am grateful for...

Today I learned...

How good am I prepared for the next day? 0 25% 50% 75% 100%

- huge pile of theory break into smaller particles -

Main Goals ☐ ☐ ☐

My Big Goal (long-term)

Additional tasks

Exams / tests 1. 2. 3.

Things I need — school supplies ☐ ☐ ☐

People I want to meet — name/reason ☐ ☐ ☐

Today's challenge ☐

My mentor's tasks 1. ☐ 2. ☐

What do I need to do to make this day great?

Today's successes

Incredible ideas

Preparation / learning plan

4:00 pm ☐
5:00 pm ☐
6:00 pm ☐
7:00 pm ☐
8:00 pm ☐
9:00 pm ☐

Efficiency of my 12 hour cycle

hours %

12 3 6 9

How do I evaluate my today's efforts? 0 25% 50% 75% 100%

Reward for meeting all my objectives

I am grateful for...

Today I learned...

How good am I prepared for the next day? 0 25% 50% 75% 100%

"I allow others to follow me!"

Main Goals ☐ ☐ ☐

My Big Goal (long-term)

Additional tasks

Exams / tests 1. 2. 3.

Things I need — school supplies ☐ ☐ ☐

People I want to meet — name/reason ☐ ☐ ☐

Today's challenge ☐

My mentor's tasks 1. ☐ 2. ☐

What do I need to do to make this day great?

Today's successes

Incredible ideas

Preparation / learning plan

4:00 pm ☐
5:00 pm ☐
6:00 pm ☐
7:00 pm ☐
8:00 pm ☐
9:00 pm ☐

Efficiency of my 12 hour cycle

hours %

12 3 6 9

How do I evaluate my today's efforts? 0 25% 50% 75% 100%

Reward for meeting all my objectives

I am grateful for...

Today I learned...

How good am I prepared for the next day? 0 25% 50% 75% 100%

- focus only on your personal outcome -

Main Goals ☐ ☐ ☐

My Big Goal (long-term)

Additional tasks

Exams / tests 1. 2. 3.

Things I need — school supplies ☐ ☐ ☐

People I want to meet — name/reason ☐ ☐ ☐

Today's challenge ☐

My mentor's tasks 1. ☐ 2. ☐

What do I need to do to make this day great?

Today's successes

Incredible ideas

Preparation / learning plan

4:00 pm ☐
5:00 pm ☐
6:00 pm ☐
7:00 pm ☐
8:00 pm ☐
9:00 pm ☐

Efficiency of my 12 hour cycle

hours %

12 3 6 9

How do I evaluate my today's efforts? 0 25% 50% 75% 100%

Reward for meeting all my objectives

I am grateful for...

Today I learned...

How good am I prepared for the next day? 0 25% 50% 75% 100%

"I believe in my potential!"

Main Goals ☐ ☐ ☐

My Big Goal (long-term)

Additional tasks

Exams / tests 1. 2. 3.

Things I need — school supplies ☐ ☐ ☐

People I want to meet — name/reason ☐ ☐ ☐

Today's challenge ☐

My mentor's tasks 1. ☐ 2. ☐

What do I need to do to make this day great?

Today's successes

Incredible ideas

Preparation / learning plan

4:00 pm ☐

5:00 pm ☐

6:00 pm ☐

7:00 pm ☐

8:00 pm ☐

9:00 pm ☐

Efficiency of my 12 hour cycle

hours %

12 3 6 9

How do I evaluate my today's efforts? 0 25% 50% 75% 100%

Reward for meeting all my objectives

I am grateful for...

Today I learned...

How good am I prepared for the next day? 0 25% 50% 75% 100%

Date __ / __ / ____ ______________

- ignore those unprepaared, they are not your problem -

Main Goals ☐ ☐ ☐

My Big Goal (long-term)

Additional tasks

Exams / tests 1. ____ 2. ____ 3. ____

Things I need — school supplies ☐ ☐ ☐

People I want to meet — name/reason ☐ ☐ ☐

Today's challenge ☐

My mentor's tasks 1. ____ ☐ 2. ____ ☐

What do I need to do to make this day great?

Today's successes

Incredible ideas

Preparation / learning plan

4:00 pm ☐

5:00 pm ☐

6:00 pm ☐

7:00 pm ☐

8:00 pm ☐

9:00 pm ☐

Efficiency of my 12 hour cycle

[ ] hours [ ] %

12 3 6 9

How do I evaluate my today's efforts? 0 25% 50% 75% 100%

Reward for meeting all my objectives

I am grateful for...

Today I learned...

How good am I prepared for the next day? 0 25% 50% 75% 100%

Date __ / __ / ____

"I'm stronger day by day!"

Main Goals ☐ ☐ ☐

My Big Goal (long-term)

Additional tasks

Exams / tests 1. 2. 3.

Things I need — school supplies ☐ ☐ ☐

People I want to meet — name/reason ☐ ☐ ☐

Today's challenge ☐

My mentor's tasks 1. ☐ 2. ☐

What do I need to do to make this day great?

Today's successes

Incredible ideas

Preparation / learning plan

4:00 pm ☐

5:00 pm ☐

6:00 pm ☐

7:00 pm ☐

8:00 pm ☐

9:00 pm ☐

Efficiency of my 12 hour cycle

hours %

12 3 6 9

How do I evaluate my today's efforts? 0 25% 50% 75% 100%

Reward for meeting all my objectives

I am grateful for...

Today I learned...

How good am I prepared for the next day? 0 25% 50% 75% 100%

Date __/__/____ ____________ LEO - Learning organizer

- 5 basic questions - Who? Where? When? How? Why? -

Main Goals ☐ ☐ ☐

My Big Goal (long-term)

Additional tasks

Exams / tests 1. 2. 3.

Things I need — school supplies ☐ ☐ ☐

People I want to meet — name/reason ☐ ☐ ☐

Today's challenge ☐

My mentor's tasks 1. ☐ 2. ☐

What do I need to do to make this day great?

Today's successes

Incredible ideas

Preparation / learning plan

4:00 pm ☐

5:00 pm ☐

6:00 pm ☐

7:00 pm ☐

8:00 pm ☐

9:00 pm ☐

Efficiency of my 12 hour cycle

hours %

12 3 6 9

How do I evaluate my today's efforts? 0 25% 50% 75% 100%

Reward for meeting all my objectives

I am grateful for...

Today I learned...

How good am I prepared for the next day? 0 25% 50% 75% 100%

Date __/__/____ ____________

"This is the right moment!"

Main Goals ☐ ☐ ☐

My Big Goal (long-term)

Additional tasks

Exams / tests 1. ______ 2. ______ 3. ______

Things I need — school supplies ☐ ☐ ☐

People I want to meet — name/reason ☐ ☐ ☐

Today's challenge ☐

My mentor's tasks 1. ______ ☐ 2. ______ ☐

What do I need to do to make this day great?

Today's successes

Incredible ideas

Preparation / learning plan

4:00 pm ☐

5:00 pm ☐

6:00 pm ☐

7:00 pm ☐

8:00 pm ☐

9:00 pm ☐

Efficiency of my 12 hour cycle ____ hours ____ %

12 3 6 9

How do I evaluate my today's efforts? 0 25% 50% 75% 100%

Reward for meeting all my objectives

I am grateful for...

Today I learned...

How good am I prepared for the next day? 0 25% 50% 75% 100%

- learn to be perfect in presentation before any oral exam -

Main Goals ☐ ☐ ☐

My Big Goal (long-term)

Additional tasks

Exams / tests 1. 2. 3.

Things I need — school supplies ☐ ☐ ☐

People I want to meet — name/reason ☐ ☐ ☐

Today's challenge ☐

My mentor's tasks 1. ☐ 2. ☐

What do I need to do to make this day great?

Today's successes

Incredible ideas

Preparation / learning plan

4:00 pm ☐
5:00 pm ☐
6:00 pm ☐
7:00 pm ☐
8:00 pm ☐
9:00 pm ☐

Efficiency of my 12 hour cycle
hours %

12 3 6 9

How do I evaluate my today's efforts? 0 25% 50% 75% 100%

Reward for meeting all my objectives

I am grateful for...

Today I learned...

How good am I prepared for the next day? 0 25% 50% 75% 100%

Date __ / __ / _____

"This day will be fantastic!"

Main Goals ☐ ☐ ☐

My Big Goal (long-term)

Additional tasks

Exams / tests 1. 2. 3.

Things I need — school supplies ☐ ☐ ☐

People I want to meet — name/reason ☐ ☐ ☐

Today's challenge ☐

My mentor's tasks 1. ☐ 2. ☐

What do I need to do to make this day great?

Today's successes

Incredible ideas

Preparation / learning plan

4:00 pm ☐
5:00 pm ☐
6:00 pm ☐
7:00 pm ☐
8:00 pm ☐
9:00 pm ☐

Efficiency of my 12 hour cycle

hours %

12 3 6 9

How do I evaluate my today's efforts? 0 25% 50% 75% 100%

Reward for meeting all my objectives

I am grateful for...

Today I learned...

How good am I prepared for the next day? 0 25% 50% 75% 100%

- if you don't have super-memory - create your own system -

Main Goals ☐ ☐ ☐

My Big Goal (long-term)

Additional tasks

Exams / tests 1. 2. 3.

Things I need — school supplies ☐ ☐ ☐

People I want to meet — name/reason ☐ ☐ ☐

Today's challenge ☐

My mentor's tasks 1. ☐ 2. ☐

What do I need to do to make this day great?

Today's successes

Incredible ideas

Preparation / learning plan

4:00 pm ☐
5:00 pm ☐
6:00 pm ☐
7:00 pm ☐
8:00 pm ☐
9:00 pm ☐

Efficiency of my 12 hour cycle

hours %

12 3 6 9

How do I evaluate my today's efforts? 0 25% 50% 75% 100%

Reward for meeting all my objectives

I am grateful for...

Today I learned...

How good am I prepared for the next day? 0 25% 50% 75% 100%

Date __/__/____ ____________

"Champion, stand up! The spotlight is in the skies!"

Main Goals ☐ ☐ ☐

My Big Goal (long-term)

Additional tasks

Exams / tests 1. 2. 3.

Things I need — school supplies ☐ ☐ ☐

People I want to meet — name/reason ☐ ☐ ☐

Today's challenge ☐

My mentor's tasks 1. ☐ 2. ☐

What do I need to do to make this day great?

Today's successes

Incredible ideas

Preparation / learning plan

4:00 pm ☐

5:00 pm ☐

6:00 pm ☐

7:00 pm ☐

8:00 pm ☐

9:00 pm ☐

Efficiency of my 12 hour cycle

hours %

12 3 6 9

How do I evaluate my today's efforts? 0 25% 50% 75% 100%

Reward for meeting all my objectives

I am grateful for...

Today I learned...

How good am I prepared for the next day? 0 25% 50% 75% 100%

- every goal should be specific and reachable -

Main Goals ☐ ☐ ☐

My Big Goal (long-term)

Additional tasks

Exams / tests 1. 2. 3.

Things I need — school supplies ☐ ☐ ☐

People I want to meet — name/reason ☐ ☐ ☐

Today's challenge ☐

My mentor's tasks 1. ☐ 2. ☐

What do I need to do to make this day great?

Today's successes

Incredible ideas

Preparation / learning plan

4:00 pm ☐

5:00 pm ☐

6:00 pm ☐

7:00 pm ☐

8:00 pm ☐

9:00 pm ☐

Efficiency of my 12 hour cycle

hours %

12 3 6 9

How do I evaluate my today's efforts? 0 25% 50% 75% 100%

Reward for meeting all my objectives

I am grateful for...

Today I learned...

How good am I prepared for the next day? 0 25% 50% 75% 100%

Date __ / __ / ____

"One step closer to my Big Goal!"

Main Goals ☐ ☐ ☐

My Big Goal (long-term)

Additional tasks

Exams / tests 1. 2. 3.

Things I need — school supplies ☐ ☐ ☐

People I want to meet — name/reason ☐ ☐ ☐

Today's challenge ☐

My mentor's tasks 1. ☐ 2. ☐

What do I need to do to make this day great?

Today's successes

Incredible ideas

Preparation / learning plan

4:00 pm ☐
5:00 pm ☐
6:00 pm ☐
7:00 pm ☐
8:00 pm ☐
9:00 pm ☐

Efficiency of my 12 hour cycle

hours %

12 3 6 9

How do I evaluate my today's efforts? 0 25% 50% 75% 100%

Reward for meeting all my objectives

I am grateful for...

Today I learned...

How good am I prepared for the next day? 0 25% 50% 75% 100%

- give yourself a reward for your successes -

Main Goals ☐ ☐ ☐

My Big Goal (long-term)

Additional tasks

Exams / tests 1. 2. 3.

Things I need — school supplies ☐ ☐ ☐

People I want to meet — name/reason ☐ ☐ ☐

Today's challenge ☐

My mentor's tasks 1. ☐ 2. ☐

What do I need to do to make this day great?

Today's successes

Incredible ideas

Preparation / learning plan

4:00 pm ☐
5:00 pm ☐
6:00 pm ☐
7:00 pm ☐
8:00 pm ☐
9:00 pm ☐

Efficiency of my 12 hour cycle

hours %

12 3 6 9

How do I evaluate my today's efforts? 0 25% 50% 75% 100%

Reward for meeting all my objectives

I am grateful for...

Today I learned...

How good am I prepared for the next day? 0 25% 50% 75% 100%

Date __/__/____

"I know my goals therefore I know which way to go!"

Main Goals ☐ ☐ ☐

My Big Goal (long-term)

Additional tasks

Exams / tests 1. 2. 3.

Things I need — school supplies ☐ ☐ ☐

People I want to meet — name/reason ☐ ☐ ☐

Today's challenge ☐

My mentor's tasks 1. ☐ 2. ☐

What do I need to do to make this day great?

Today's successes

Incredible ideas

Preparation / learning plan

4:00 pm ☐

5:00 pm ☐

6:00 pm ☐

7:00 pm ☐

8:00 pm ☐

9:00 pm ☐

Efficiency of my 12 hour cycle

hours %

12 3 6 9

How do I evaluate my today's efforts? 0 25% 50% 75% 100%

Reward for meeting all my objectives

I am grateful for...

Today I learned...

How good am I prepared for the next day? 0 25% 50% 75% 100%

- is there any reason why you shouldn't be an A-student? -

Main Goals ☐ ☐ ☐

My Big Goal (long-term)

Additional tasks

Exams / tests 1. 2. 3.

Things I need — school supplies ☐ ☐ ☐

People I want to meet — name/reason ☐ ☐ ☐

Today's challenge ☐

My mentor's tasks 1. ☐ 2. ☐

What do I need to do to make this day great?

Today's successes

Incredible ideas

Preparation / learning plan

4:00 pm ☐

5:00 pm ☐

6:00 pm ☐

7:00 pm ☐

8:00 pm ☐

9:00 pm ☐

Efficiency of my 12 hour cycle

hours %

12 3 6 9

How do I evaluate my today's efforts? 0 25% 50% 75% 100%

Reward for meeting all my objectives

I am grateful for...

Today I learned...

How good am I prepared for the next day? 0 25% 50% 75% 100%

"My preparation is bulletproof!"

Main Goals ☐ ☐ ☐

My Big Goal (long-term)

Additional tasks

Exams / tests 1. 2. 3.

Things I need — school supplies ☐ ☐ ☐

People I want to meet — name/reason ☐ ☐ ☐

Today's challenge ☐

My mentor's tasks 1. ☐ 2. ☐

What do I need to do to make this day great?

Today's successes

Incredible ideas

Preparation / learning plan

4:00 pm ☐
5:00 pm ☐
6:00 pm ☐
7:00 pm ☐
8:00 pm ☐
9:00 pm ☐

Efficiency of my 12 hour cycle

hours %

12 3 6 9

How do I evaluate my today's efforts? 0 25% 50% 75% 100%

Reward for meeting all my objectives

I am grateful for...

Today I learned...

How good am I prepared for the next day? 0 25% 50% 75% 100%

- be bold to have Big Dreams -

Main Goals ☐ ☐ ☐

My Big Goal (long-term)

Additional tasks

Exams / tests 1. 2. 3.

Things I need — school supplies ☐ ☐ ☐

People I want to meet — name/reason ☐ ☐ ☐

Today's challenge ☐

My mentor's tasks 1. ☐ 2. ☐

What do I need to do to make this day great?

Today's successes

Incredible ideas

Preparation / learning plan

4:00 pm ☐

5:00 pm ☐

6:00 pm ☐

7:00 pm ☐

8:00 pm ☐

9:00 pm ☐

Efficiency of my 12 hour cycle

hours %

12 3 6 9

How do I evaluate my today's efforts? 0 25% 50% 75% 100%

Reward for meeting all my objectives

I am grateful for...

Today I learned...

How good am I prepared for the next day? 0 25% 50% 75% 100%

Date __/__/____

"I need to think and learn the easy way!"

Main Goals ☐ ☐ ☐

My Big Goal (long-term)

Additional tasks

Exams / tests 1. 2. 3.

Things I need — school supplies ☐ ☐ ☐

People I want to meet — name/reason ☐ ☐ ☐

Today's challenge ☐

My mentor's tasks 1. ☐ 2. ☐

What do I need to do to make this day great?

Today's successes

Incredible ideas

Preparation / learning plan

4:00 pm ☐

5:00 pm ☐

6:00 pm ☐

7:00 pm ☐

8:00 pm ☐

9:00 pm ☐

Efficiency of my 12 hour cycle

hours %

12 3 6 9

How do I evaluate my today's efforts? 0 25% 50% 75% 100%

Reward for meeting all my objectives

I am grateful for...

Today I learned...

How good am I prepared for the next day? 0 25% 50% 75% 100%

Date __/__/____ ____________

- decide on what do you want and what do you can achieve -

Main Goals ☐ ☐ ☐

My Big Goal (long-term)

Additional tasks

Exams / tests 1. ______ 2. ______ 3. ______

Things I need — school supplies ☐ ☐ ☐

People I want to meet — name/reason ☐ ☐ ☐

Today's challenge ☐

My mentor's tasks 1. ______ ☐ 2. ______ ☐

What do I need to do to make this day great?

Today's successes

Incredible ideas

Preparation / learning plan

4:00 pm ☐

5:00 pm ☐

6:00 pm ☐

7:00 pm ☐

8:00 pm ☐

9:00 pm ☐

Efficiency of my 12 hour cycle

[ ] hours [ ] %

12 3 6 9

How do I evaluate my today's efforts? 0 25% 50% 75% 100%

Reward for meeting all my objectives

I am grateful for...

Today I learned...

How good am I prepared for the next day? 0 25% 50% 75% 100%

Date __/__/____

"I can do it!"

Main Goals ☐ ☐ ☐

My Big Goal (long-term)

Additional tasks

Exams / tests 1. 2. 3.

Things I need — school supplies ☐ ☐ ☐

People I want to meet — name/reason ☐ ☐ ☐

Today's challenge ☐

My mentor's tasks 1. ☐ 2. ☐

What do I need to do to make this day great?

Today's successes

Incredible ideas

Preparation / learning plan

4:00 pm ☐
5:00 pm ☐
6:00 pm ☐
7:00 pm ☐
8:00 pm ☐
9:00 pm ☐

Efficiency of my 12 hour cycle

hours %

12 3 6 9

How do I evaluate my today's efforts? 0 25% 50% 75% 100%

Reward for meeting all my objectives

I am grateful for...

Today I learned...

How good am I prepared for the next day? 0 25% 50% 75% 100%

- your reward is waiting for you -

Main Goals ☐ ☐ ☐

My Big Goal (long-term)

Additional tasks

Exams / tests 1. 2. 3.

Things I need — school supplies ☐ ☐ ☐

People I want to meet — name/reason ☐ ☐ ☐

Today's challenge ☐

My mentor's tasks 1. ☐ 2. ☐

What do I need to do to make this day great?

Today's successes

Incredible ideas

Preparation / learning plan

4:00 pm ☐

5:00 pm ☐

6:00 pm ☐

7:00 pm ☐

8:00 pm ☐

9:00 pm ☐

Efficiency of my 12 hour cycle

hours %

12 3 6 9

How do I evaluate my today's efforts? 0 25% 50% 75% 100%

Reward for meeting all my objectives

I am grateful for...

Today I learned...

How good am I prepared for the next day? 0 25% 50% 75% 100%

"Nothing can stop me!"

Main Goals ☐ ☐ ☐

My Big Goal (long-term)

Additional tasks

Exams / tests 1. 2. 3.

Things I need school supplies ☐ ☐ ☐

People I want to meet name/reason ☐ ☐ ☐

Today's challenge ☐

My mentor's tasks 1. ☐ 2. ☐

What do I need to do to make this day great?

Today's successes

Incredible ideas

Preparation / learning plan

4:00 pm ☐
5:00 pm ☐
6:00 pm ☐
7:00 pm ☐
8:00 pm ☐
9:00 pm ☐

Efficiency of my 12 hour cycle
hours %

12 3 6 9

How do I evaluate my today's efforts? 0 25% 50% 75% 100%

Reward for meeting all my objectives

I am grateful for...

Today I learned...

How good am I prepared for the next day? 0 25% 50% 75% 100%

- you don't want to stop now -

Main Goals ☐ ☐ ☐

My Big Goal (long-term)

Additional tasks

Exams / tests 1. 2. 3.

Things I need — school supplies ☐ ☐ ☐

People I want to meet — name/reason ☐ ☐ ☐

Today's challenge ☐

My mentor's tasks 1. ☐ 2. ☐

What do I need to do to make this day great?

Today's successes

Incredible ideas

Preparation / learning plan

4:00 pm ☐

5:00 pm ☐

6:00 pm ☐

7:00 pm ☐

8:00 pm ☐

9:00 pm ☐

Efficiency of my 12 hour cycle

hours %

12 3 6 9

How do I evaluate my today's efforts? 0 25% 50% 75% 100%

Reward for meeting all my objectives

I am grateful for...

Today I learned...

How good am I prepared for the next day? 0 25% 50% 75% 100%

"Being better everyday is in my nature!"

Main Goals ☐ ☐ ☐

My Big Goal (long-term)

Additional tasks

Exams / tests 1. 2. 3.

Things I need — school supplies ☐ ☐ ☐

People I want to meet — name/reason ☐ ☐ ☐

Today's challenge ☐

My mentor's tasks 1. ☐ 2. ☐

What do I need to do to make this day great?

Today's successes

Incredible ideas

Preparation / learning plan

4:00 pm ☐
5:00 pm ☐
6:00 pm ☐
7:00 pm ☐
8:00 pm ☐
9:00 pm ☐

Efficiency of my 12 hour cycle

hours %

12 3 6 9

How do I evaluate my today's efforts? 0 25% 50% 75% 100%

Reward for meeting all my objectives

I am grateful for...

Today I learned...

How good am I prepared for the next day? 0 25% 50% 75% 100%

- you are in the control of your emotions -

Main Goals ☐ ☐ ☐

My Big Goal (long-term)

Additional tasks

Exams / tests 1. 2. 3.

Things I need — school supplies ☐ ☐ ☐

People I want to meet — name/reason ☐ ☐ ☐

Today's challenge ☐

My mentor's tasks 1. ☐ 2. ☐

What do I need to do to make this day great?

Today's successes

Incredible ideas

Preparation / learning plan

4:00 pm ☐

5:00 pm ☐

6:00 pm ☐

7:00 pm ☐

8:00 pm ☐

9:00 pm ☐

Efficiency of my 12 hour cycle

hours %

12 3 6 9

How do I evaluate my today's efforts? 0 25% 50% 75% 100%

Reward for meeting all my objectives

I am grateful for...

Today I learned...

How good am I prepared for the next day? 0 25% 50% 75% 100%

Date __/__/____

"I can control myself!"

Main Goals ☐ ☐ ☐

My Big Goal (long-term)

Additional tasks

Exams / tests 1. 2. 3.

Things I need — school supplies ☐ ☐ ☐

People I want to meet — name/reason ☐ ☐ ☐

Today's challenge ☐

My mentor's tasks 1. ☐ 2. ☐

What do I need to do to make this day great?

Today's successes

Incredible ideas

Preparation / learning plan

4:00 pm ☐

5:00 pm ☐

6:00 pm ☐

7:00 pm ☐

8:00 pm ☐

9:00 pm ☐

Efficiency of my 12 hour cycle

hours %

12 3 6 9

How do I evaluate my today's efforts? 0 25% 50% 75% 100%

Reward for meeting all my objectives

I am grateful for...

Today I learned...

How good am I prepared for the next day? 0 25% 50% 75% 100%

Date __ / __ / ____

– your preparation is essential for your success –

Main Goals ☐ ☐ ☐

My Big Goal (long-term)

Additional tasks

Exams / tests 1. 2. 3.

Things I need — school supplies ☐ ☐ ☐

People I want to meet — name/reason ☐ ☐ ☐

Today's challenge ☐

My mentor's tasks 1. ☐ 2. ☐

What do I need to do to make this day great?

Today's successes

Incredible ideas

Preparation / learning plan

4:00 pm ☐
5:00 pm ☐
6:00 pm ☐
7:00 pm ☐
8:00 pm ☐
9:00 pm ☐

Efficiency of my 12 hour cycle
hours %

12 3 6 9

How do I evaluate my today's efforts? 0 25% 50% 75% 100%

Reward for meeting all my objectives

I am grateful for...

Today I learned...

How good am I prepared for the next day? 0 25% 50% 75% 100%

Date __/__/____

"I am calm!"

Main Goals ☐ ☐ ☐

My Big Goal (long-term)

Additional tasks

Exams / tests 1. 2. 3.

Things I need — school supplies ☐ ☐ ☐

People I want to meet — name/reason ☐ ☐ ☐

Today's challenge ☐

My mentor's tasks 1. ☐ 2. ☐

What do I need to do to make this day great?

Today's successes

Incredible ideas

Preparation / learning plan

4:00 pm ☐

5:00 pm ☐

6:00 pm ☐

7:00 pm ☐

8:00 pm ☐

9:00 pm ☐

Efficiency of my 12 hour cycle

hours %

12 3 6 9

How do I evaluate my today's efforts? 0 25% 50% 75% 100%

Reward for meeting all my objectives

I am grateful for...

Today I learned...

How good am I prepared for the next day? 0 25% 50% 75% 100%

- congratulations, you've made it! -

Main Goals ☐ ☐ ☐

My Big Goal (long-term)

Additional tasks

Exams / tests 1. 2. 3.

Things I need — school supplies ☐ ☐ ☐

People I want to meet — name/reason ☐ ☐ ☐

Today's challenge ☐

My mentor's tasks 1. ☐ 2. ☐

What do I need to do to make this day great?

Today's successes

Incredible ideas

Preparation / learning plan

4:00 pm ☐

5:00 pm ☐

6:00 pm ☐

7:00 pm ☐

8:00 pm ☐

9:00 pm ☐

Efficiency of my 12 hour cycle

hours %

12 3 6 9

How do I evaluate my today's efforts? 0 25% 50% 75% 100%

Reward for meeting all my objectives

I am grateful for...

Today I learned...

How good am I prepared for the next day? 0 25% 50% 75% 100%

Understand your possibilities!

Learn to know your inborn abilities - let yourself diagnose by licensed psychological institute; eg. personality, intelligence. The results will tell you about your strong, average or weak elements of your personality, intelligence, emotions, etc.

The Personality Tests Results

strong element

weak element

The Inteligency Tests Results

strong element

weak element

Other Results

Free your mind

What are the 3 most precious thoughts that you allow to enter into your mind in last seconds before THE TEST?

Write down the most common positive thoughts you have when you're facing the test. Reduce them 3 times so at the end you'll have just 3 most important of them. This will make your choice easier when facing real challenge. Reject all negative thoughts!!!

In the school bag checklist

GENERIC / LEARNING BAG

- ball point pens/biros
- pencils
- crayons/highlighters
- calculator
- rubber
- color stickers
- books, learning material
- special accesories

EXAM / TEST BAG

Always have backup pens available!

- 2 blue ballpoint pens / biros
- colored pens
- 2 pencils / propelling pencils
- crayons/highlighters
- calculator
- snack
- liquids
- books
- accesories
  - rubber
  - refill cartridges
  - rullers
  - compass
- special accesories
  - laptop
  - mobile phone
  - glasses
- library / gym membership cards

List of mistakes (fails, weak aspects)

fixed

fixed

Write the mistakes or weak aspects of your performance during tests, oral exams, learning, etc. Work hard on correcting them. **Repair & never repeat!**

Custom strategies for achieving goals

Strategy for the subject with F or worse grade at the last semster's evaluation (achieved in___months)

- ☐ find yourself a mentor (succesful person, teacher, etc.)
- ☐ get___or more D's
- ☐ first meeting with your mentor

Strategy for the subject with grade D at the last semster's evaluation (achieved in___months)

- ☐ learn___words from the language you always wanted but never started to learn
- ☐ get___or more C's
- ☐ ___productive meetings with your mentor

Strategy for the subject with grade C at the last semster's evaluation (achieved in___months)

- ☐ ___or more own attempts for oral exam
- ☐ fulfill___goal your mentor set for yourself
- ☐ learn___words from the language you always wanted but never started to learn
- ☐ get___or more B's
- ☐ get___or less C's or worse grades
- ☐ ___productive meetings with your mentor
- ☐ exercise___minutes a day, at least___days in a week (physical workout)

Strategy for the subject with grade B at the last semster's evaluation (achieved in___months)

- ☐ ___or more own attempts for oral exam
- ☐ fulfill___goal your mentor set for yourself
- ☐ learn___words from the language you always wanted but never started to learn
- ☐ get___or more A's
- ☐ get___or less B's or worse grades
- ☐ ___productive meetings with your mentor
- ☐ exercise___minutes a day, at least___days in a week (physical workout)

Strategy for the overall exemplary evaluation in the forthcoming semster (achieved in___months)

- ▢ ___or more own attempts for oral exam
- ▢ fulfill___goal your mentor set for yourself
- ▢ learn___words from the language you always wanted but never started to learn
- ▢ get___or more A's
- ▢ get___or less B's or worse grades
- ▢ ___productive meeting with your mentor
- ▢ exercise___minutes a day, at least___days in a week (physical workout)
- ▢ ___extra task 1. ____________________
- ▢ ___extra task 2. ____________________

Evaluation & Improvement

100%	A+	95%	A	90%	B	80%	C	70%	D	60%	Fx

Written exams % (monthly overview)

	1. month	2. m	3. m	4. m	5. m	6. m	7. m	8. m	9. m	10. m
indicator										
results										

school year %

	previous	actual
indicator		
per year		

Oral exams % (monthly overview)

	1. month	2. m	3. m	4. m	5. m	6. m	7. m	8. m	9. m	10. m
indicator										
results										

school year %

	previous	actual
indicator		
per year		

Combined written vs. oral exams % (monthly overview)

	1. month	2. m	3. m	4. m	5. m	6. m	7. m	8. m	9. m	10. m
indicator										
results										

school year %

	previous	actual
indicator		
per year		

Keep tracking monthly percentage of all evaluations from all your main subjects. Record your written as well as oral exam evaluation percentage.

RECORD, ANALYZE & PROGRESS!

examples		
indicator	↓	↑
%	71,4	91,7

indicator depends on how you performed in previous month